SOUTHERN
STEAM
in camera

John Adams and
Patrick Whitehouse

LONDON
IAN ALLAN LTD

First published 1977

ISBN 0 7110 0811 6

Published by Ian Allan Ltd, Shepperton, Surrey,
and printed in the United Kingdom by
Ian Allan Printing Ltd.

Above: Down Ramsgate express approaching Dumpton
Park in April 1957. The locomotive is 'Schools' class 4-4-0
No 30926 *Repton./P B Whitehouse*

Right: The Wenford Bridge branch, 1959: ex-LSWR
Beattie 2-4-0WT No 30587./*P M Alexander*

Introduction

Perhaps the Southern Region's greatest charm for the railway enthusiast was its great variety of steam engine types, ranging from ancient Beattie tanks in Cornwall to Bulleid's Pacifics with their streamlined casings and enclosed chain-driven valve gear.

The old constituent companies making up the Southern Railway of 1923 were mainly passenger lines. Of these, only the London & South Western had trains which could be called long-distance expresses; hence the SR group owned a large number of tank engine types and classes, of varying vintage, for use in Kent and Sussex in particular. The Southern even inherited island railways in the three companies which served the Isle of Wight.

By the date of Nationalisation, 1948, the overall policy for the eastern network was one of electrification. This either prevented or excused the locomotive authorities from introducing anything new in the form of tank engines and, indeed, only one class of freight engine. Passenger locomotives, too, tended to be of pre-grouping vintage, bar the 'Lord Nelsons' and, later, Bulleid's revolutionary Pacifics and the dreadful-looking Q1 goods. Thus the 1950s, and even the early 1960s, produced a fine selection of motive power, much of it in varying degrees of antiquity. There were Victorian Stroudley 'Terrier' tanks working the Hayling Island branch, old Adams 0-4-4 tanks in the Isle of Wight, Adams 4-4-2 tanks on the twisting line to Lyme Regis and antique shunters at Southampton Docks. The regular use of the Maunsell rebuilds of the SE&CR D and E class 4-4-0s, plus the later Ls and L1s, gave the inside-cylindered 4-4-0 its last hard (and successful) fling, mostly in Kent — indeed the grand 'Night Ferry' express was often double-headed with a Bulleid Pacific and an L1. On

Above: 'Merchant Navy' Pacific No 35028 *Clan Line* at the coaling stage of Nine Elms MPD./*Eric Treacy*

Above right: Ex-LB&SCR 4-4-2 tank No 26 as Southern Railway Class I3 No 2026 on an Eastbourne to Tunbridge Wells train near Groombridge in 1948. These engines were built by Marsh between 1907 and 1913; the last of the class was withdrawn in 1952./*P M Alexander*

the other hand some of Britain's most modern locomotives were hard at work on the longer distance expresses in the form of the Jarvis-designed rebuilt Bulleid engines one of which, *Ellerman Line,* now rests, sectioned, in the National Railway Museum at York while another, *Clan Line,* still works the occasional enthusiasts' special. The other outstanding engines were the three-cylinder 'Schools' class 4-4-0s — the final and most powerful design to that wheel arrangement to be found in Britain.

All in all the Southern provided interest and even excitement right up to the summer of 1967, when steam finally finished with the electrification of the main line from Waterloo to Bournemouth. Some Southern steam still lives. The Bluebell Railway out of Horsted Keynes in Sussex is a preserved and living example of what it really *was* like and its engines cover the three big pre-grouping companies. What is more, there is even one of Bulleid's unrebuilt 'West Country' 4-6-2s, so perhaps Southern steam is not dead after all.

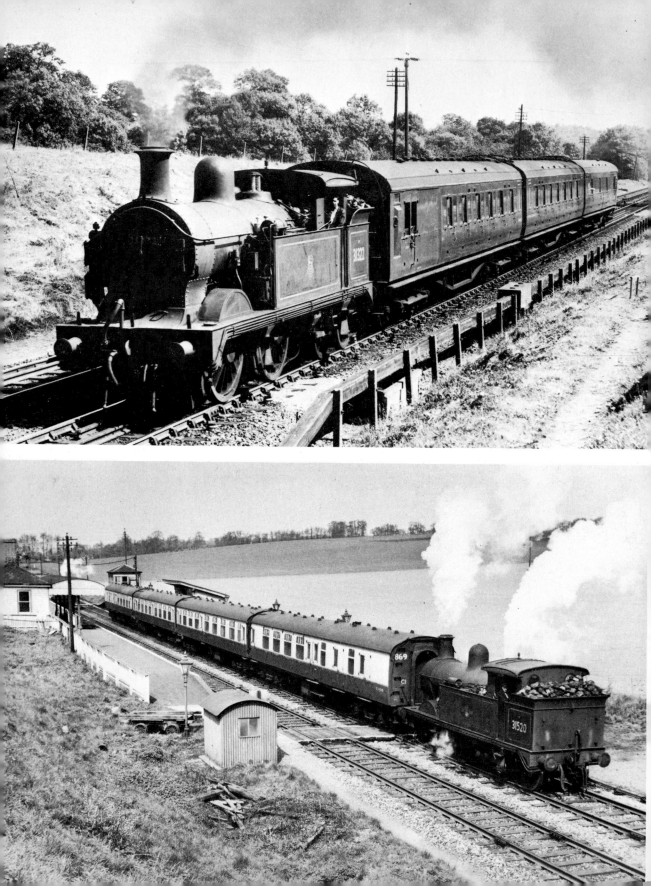

Above left: Class H 0-4-4T, BR No 31322, with a down stopping train near Weald in 1961./*Derek Cross*

Left: Another Class H 0-4-4T as BR No 31520 with a London to Allhallows excursion train at Sharnal Street in April 1960./*Derek Cross*

Above: An Oxted to Tonbridge train at Ashurst in June 1960; the engine is ex-SE&CR Class H 0-4-4T No 31521./*Derek Cross*

Wadhurst, Sussex, 20 September 1952: the first of the
'Schools' class 4-4-0s, No 30900 *Eton,* on the 1.25pm
Charing Cross to Hastings train./*P M Alexander*

Above left: An ex-SE&CR Class H 0-4-4T, BR No 31520, at Westerham./*Derek Cross*

Above: Ex-SE&CR Class F1 4-4-0 No 1156 on shed at Reading, 1 March 1947./*P M Alexander*

Left: Tonbridge to Brighton train leaving Tunbridge Wells West behind Class L 4-4-0 No 31776./*Derek Cross*

11

Left: Wadhurst, 18 September 1952: 'Schools' class 4-4-0 No 30902 *Wellington* on the 7.40am Hastings to Cannon Street express./*P M Alexander*

Below left: During the 1950s the 'Night Ferry' was often double-headed by a Maunsell Class L1 4-4-0. Here is No 31754 leading 'Battle of Britain' class 4-6-2 No 34070 *Manston* past Bickley Junction on the up train./*Derek Cross*

Above: Class N 2-6-0 No 31403 heads a down freight near Chilham./*Derek Cross*

Below: Class E 4-4-0 No 1273 (ex-SE&CR No 273) on the mid-day train from Reading to Redhill via Guildford at Shalford./*P M Alexander*

Right: Ex-SE&CR Class D 4-4-0 No 31477 stands in Wye station with a Margate to London stopping train in June 1951./*Derek Cross*

Below: Near Wadhurst, 15 September 1952: 'Schools' class 4-4-0 No 30907 *Dulwich* on the 11.28am Tonbridge to Hastings stopping train./*P M Alexander*

Below right: The final version of the SE&CR 4-4-0 — Maunsell's Class L1 No 31758 takes a Charing Cross to Ramsgate train past Dumpton Park in April 1957./*P B Whitehouse*

Left: Lyndhurst Road, 4 April 1953. Southern Class L1 4-4-0 No 31786 on a Bournemouth to Southampton stopping train./*P M Alexander*

Below left: Maunsell's rebuild of the Wainwright class D 4-4-0: Class D1 No 31487 with a Hastings line train at Tonbridge in 1961./*Derek Cross*

Above: 'Schools' class 4-4-0 No 30935 *Sevenoaks* at Ramsgate shed in 1956./*P B Whitehouse*

Below: Rebuilt 'Battle of Britain' class 4-6-2 No 34077 *603 Squadron* passing Paddock Wood in 1961./*Derek Cross*

Above: During the 1950s the ex-SE&CR 0-6-0 tanks on the Folkestone Harbour branch were replaced by Swindon-designed 0-6-0 pannier tanks. No 4601 pilots No 4616 up the hill with a boat train in 1960./*Derek Cross*

Above right: Andover Junction, 11 April 1953: BR Standard Class 2MT 2-6-2T No 41293. These LMS-design engines were also used on the Eastleigh — Romsey — Andover line./*P M Alexander*

Right: Bulleid's 'Battle of Britain' class 4-6-2 No 34086 *219 Squadron* with the down 'Golden Arrow' (diverted via Maidstone East) at Otford in March 1960./*Derek Cross*

Above: Bursledon, 2 June 1951: Southern class U1 2-6-0 No 31892 on a Brighton to Bournemouth train. */P M Alexander*

Above right: Cosham, 1 December 1951: Class H15 4-6-0 No 30490 (ex-LSWR No 490 built Eastleigh 1914) on the heavily-loaded Portsmouth to Eastleigh vans (15 eight-wheel bogies and 9 four-wheel vehicles). */P M Alexander*

Right: Near Brockenhurst, 19 April 1954: Class H15 4-6-0 No 30491 (the only one of the class fitted with N15-type boiler) on a Bournemouth to Southampton stopping train in the heart of the New Forest./*P M Alexander*

Left: Cosham, 29 October 1951: Class H15 4-6-0 No 30477 (ex-LSWR No 477 built Eastleigh 1924) with the vans and empty stock train from Portsmouth Harbour to Salisbury via Eastleigh. This train was usually heavily loaded and on this day it had 11 four-wheel vans and 17 assorted four- and six-wheelers./*P M Alexander*

Below left: Basingstoke, 25 September 1949: Class 4-6-0 No 30741 *Joyous Gard,* in Brunswick green and fitted with Lemaître blast-pipe and large diameter chimney. /*P M Alexander*

Above: Class N15 4-6-0 No 30784 *Sir Nerovens* with a Weymouth to Eastleigh train on 2 January 1951. /*P M Alexander*

Below: Winchfield, 10 June 1950: 'King Arthur' class 4-6-0 No 30455 *Sir Launcelot* on the Nine Elms to Southampton Docks milk train via East Putney. /*P M Alexander*

Rebuilt *'West Country'* class 4-6-2 No 34003 *Plymouth* at Sandling Junction in 1961./*Derek Cross*

Above: Guildford, 14 November 1949: Class H16 4-6-2T No 30516 pulling away with great vigour on the Nine Elms freight./*P M Alexander*

Below: Eastleigh, 9 April 1950: Class Z 0-8-0T No 30950./*P M Alexander*

Right: Shalford, 1 January 1951: Ex-WD 2-8-0 No 90360 in BR livery, pulling away from a signal check at Shalford Junction with a Reading to Redhill freight. /*P M Alexander*

Below right: Guildford, 19 June 1951: Ex-LSWR '0395' class 0-6-0 No 30577 and Class U1 2-6-0 No 31625. /*P M Alexander*

Above: Brighton, 18 July 1951: BR Standard 4-6-2 No 70014 *Iron Duke* (home shed, Nine Elms) visiting Brighton works for minor adjustments. This was believed to be the first appearance of a class 7 Pacific at Brighton./*P M Alexander*

Above right: Southampton, 27 January 1951: 'West Country' class 4-6-2 No 34094 *Mortehoe* on the 12.40am Bournemouth to Waterloo. Note the RMS *Queen Elizabeth* beneath the bridge, left background. /*P M Alexander*

Right: Between Farnborough and Pirbright Junction, 15 September 1951: 'West Country' class 4-6-2 No 34012 *Launceston* on the 1.15pm Bournemouth to Waterloo express./*P M Alexander*

Above left: Southampton, 27 January 1951: 'Merchant Navy' class 4-6-2 No 35018 *British India Line* (in blue livery) on the 10.30am Bournemouth to Waterloo. */P M Alexander*

Left: Ashurst, 4 April 1953: Class H15 4-6-0 No 30473 on the 12.10pm train from Southampton to Bournemouth. */P M Alexander*

Above: Brookwood, 15 September 1951: Class N15 4-6-0 No 30457 *Sir Bedivere* stopping with the 3.54pm Waterloo to Basingstoke semi-fast./*P M Alexander*

Above: Liss, Hants, 30 May 1949: (ex-SE&CR) Class C 0-6-0 No 1294 on the 7.7pm freight from Petersfield to Guildford, approaching the foot of the 1 in 80 incline./*P M Alexander*

Below: The Drummond K10 class 4-4-0 emerged from Eastleigh works in 1901 and rather surprisingly lasted fifty years in service to 1951: in fact the first of the 40 engines was not taken out of service until 1947. Still with her old LSWR number, K10 No 142 stands on Fratton shed in 1949./*P M Alexander*

Above right: Hayling Island train headed by ex-LB&SCR 0-6-0 'Terrier' tank, BR No 32661./*P M Alexander*

Right: Peasmarsh Junction (Guildford), 19 July 1949: Class D3/M 0-4-4T No 32372 on the 6.7pm from Guildford to Horsham. Coaching stock is in the new BR red livery just adopted for suburban coaches. Note also mile-post 55½ via the ex-LB&SCR route; from this point to London via the ex-LSWR route is only 32 miles./*P M Alexander*

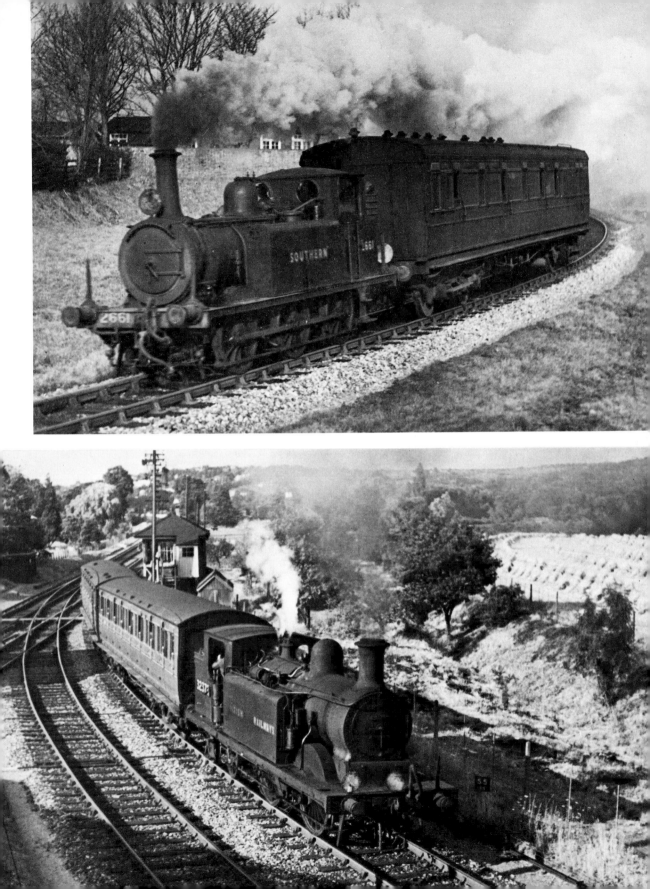

Left: West Meon, 17 September 1951: Ex-LSWR Class L12 4-4-0 No 30434 on the Alton to Fareham pick-up goods via the Meon Valley line./*P M Alexander*

Above: Class T9 4-4-0 No 30115, converted to oil-burning, on a through train from Bristol to Portsmouth at Fareham./*P M Alexander*

Below: Meon Valley Line, 12 October 1951: ex-LSWR Class T9 4-4-0 No 30313 between Privett and West Meon with the daily pick-up goods from Alton to Fareham. /*P M Alexander*

Above left: Shalford Junction (Guildford), 20 June 1949: Class K10 4-4-0 No 141 (fitted with stovepipe chimney) working the 6.42am freight from Guildford to Godalming, the duty on which she ended her days. */P M Alexander*

Above: Ash Junction, 5 June 1951: ex-LSWR Class L12 4-4-0 No 30434 on the 12.47pm Reading to Guildford. The single line branch diverging to the left is the spur connecting direct to the Farnham line, used by freight trains avoiding Aldershot./*P M Alexander*

Left: Shawford Junction, near Winchester: Class M7 0-4-4T No 30033 on a Didcot-Newbury-Southampton train. St Catherines Hill is in the background. */P M Alexander*

Left: Southampton, 27 January 1951: 'Lord Nelson' class 4-6-0 No 30855 *Robert Blake* on the 2.27pm Southampton to Bournemouth./*P M Alexander*

Below left: The Southern's largest express design was the 'Lord Nelson' 4-6-0 of 1926. No 855 *Robert Blake*, painted and lettered in a new SR style, was on Battersea shed in 1939. The engine was fitted with multiple-jet blastpipe and large-diameter chimney./*P M Alexander*

Above: Ashurst, 4 April 1953: 'Lord Nelson' 4-6-0 No 30854 *Howard of Effingham* on the 9.30am Waterloo to Bournemouth express, composed of the original experimental BR "plum-and-spilt-milk" liveried stock./*P M Alexander*

Below: 'Lord Nelson' class 4-6-0 No 30857 *Lord Howe*, with small driving wheels./*J M Jarvis*

Class D1 4-4-0 No 31735 emerges from Elmstead Woods
tunnel with a Kent Coast train./*Derek Cross*

Above left: Alton, 2 December 1951: The south end of the station, showing Class M7 0-4-4T No 30128 waiting to depart on the 12.4 (Sundays) to Winchester and Eastleigh./*P M Alexander*

Left: Fareham, 1 November 1951: Class N 2-6-0 No 31851 on an Eastleigh to Fratton goods emerging from the tunnel on the single line between Fareham and Knowle Junction. There is an alternative loop of double line 'over the hill' with 1 in 100 gradient./*P M Alexander*

Above: Ash Junction, 25 July 1951: Class M7 0-4-4T No 30026 on the 12.47pm Reading South to Guildford train./*P M Alexander*

Above left: Guildford, 3 October 1949: ex-LSWR 0-4-0ST
Ironside./P M Alexander

Above: Freshwater, IOW, 17 April 1949: Class O2
0-4-4T No 25 *Godshill,* one of the two Isle of Wight O2
locomotives fitted with Drummond
boiler./*P M Alexander*

Left: Corfe Castle village, 16 October 1965: the train is
from Swanage to Wareham, hauled by LMS-designed
Class 2 2-6-2T No 41224./*M J Fox*

Right: Ventnor Town, Isle of Wight, 27 September 1963: Class O2 0-4-4T No 20 *Shanklin* watering./*G D King*

Below: Ventnor Town, Isle of Wight. Class O2 0-4-4T No 15 *Cowes* arriving on an early morning train from Ryde Pier./*P M Alexander*

Far right: Adams designed the B4 0-4-0 tank for the LSWR in 1891 and the engines were duly built at Nine Elms. The class was extended as K14 by Drummond in 1908. Used largely as dock shunters these useful engines remained in service until 1963. B4 No 87 was photographed on Bournemouth shed in 1950. /*P M Alexander*

Below right: Ex-LSWR Beattie 2-4-0WT No 30585 near Helland on the Wenford Bridge Branch daily goods from Wadebridge in September 1959./*Derek Cross*

Right: Through coaches from Waterloo to Lyme Regis working down the branch behind two ex-LSWR '0415' class 4-4-2 tanks. Two coaches were the normal local for one of these engines over the steeply graded branch./*Ivo Peters*

Below: Axminster Station: June 1960./*John Adams*

Below right: 'West Country' class 4-6-2 No 34011 *Tavistock* heads the 'Devon Belle' Pullman train near Coleford on 28 June 1949./*C F H Oldham*

Left: Torrington, 17 May 1950: Class E1/R 0-6-2T No 32095 on the 1.0pm mixed train to the Clay Pits near Peters Marland. Gradient 1 in 67./*P M Alexander*

Below left: A train from Halwill to Barnstaple on the viaduct over the river Torridge at Torrington, headed by Class E1/R 0-6-2T No 32696.

Above: Eastleigh shed, 9 April 1950: Ex-LSWR Class M7 0-4-4T No 30040./*P M Alexander*

Below: Class N 2-6-0 No 31832 at Exeter (St Davids) on 23 June 1950./*C F H Oldham*

Below: The 5.31pm to Reading climbing out of Redhill on 23 April 1963. The engine is No 31864./*G D King*

Right: Ashurst Walk, 3 April 1953: BR Standard Class 4MT 2-6-0 No 76009 on a Southampton to Bournemouth all-stations train./*P M Alexander*

Below right: Exeter, 31 August 1949: Class M7 0-4-4T No 30374 piloting 'West Country' class 4-6-2 No 34041 *Wilton* up the 1 in 37 on an up Meldon Quarry ballast train, banked in the rear by Class E1/R 0-6-2Ts Nos 2124 and 2135./*P M Alexander*

Above left: Selsdon, 19 August 1950: Class H2 4-4-2 No 32421 *South Foreland* on the 6.58 from Brighton. /*P M Alexander*

Left: Eastleigh locomotive shed on 4 September, 1950: Class D15 4-4-0 No 30471./*P M Alexander*

Above: Fareham, 1 November 1951: Class D15 4-4-0 No 30470 on the through train Bristol to Portsmouth crossing the viaduct over the estuary of the little Wallington River, where it flows into a corner of Portsmouth Harbour./*P M Alexander*

Left: Selsdon, 18 August 1950: Ex-LB&SCR Class I3 4-4-2T No 32029 on an up train from Brighton to Victoria via Eridge./*P M Alexander*

Below left: The preserved LB&SCR 'Terrier' *Boxhill* (now in the National Railway Museum at York) at Guildford./*P M Alexander*

Below: As Service Dept No 377S old No 635 is seen here in Stroudley's "improved engine green" at Brighton works in 1948 together with Stroudley Class D1 0-4-2 tank No 2235 (fitted with a Drummond chimney). /*P M Alexander*

Above left: Ex-LB&SCR Class C2X 0-6-0 No 32535, with twin-domed boiler, on an up vans train from Tunbridge Wells, in August 1950./*P M Alexander*

Left: Elstead, 26 March 1949: Class D1/M 0-4-2T No 2252 (ex *Buckhurst,* built 1881) on a Petersfield to Midhurst train./*P M Alexander*

Above: Fareham, 24 October 1951: Class K 2-6-0 No 32349 heads the Eastleigh to Fratton goods, on the single line between Knowle Junction and Fareham. There is an alternative line (double) 'over the hill' between the same two points./*P M Alexander*

Above: Near Wadhurst, 18 September 1952: Bulleid Class Q1 0-6-0 No 33031 tackling the 1 in 75 gradient up to Wadhurst Tunnel with an up freight./*P M Alexander*

Above right: Three Bridges train arriving at East Grinstead in February 1963 behind Class H 0-4-4T No 31518./*G D King*

Right: Guildford, 22 April 1948: Class F1 4-4-0 No 1028 on the 5.5pm from Reading terminating at Guildford. /*P M Alexander*

Left: BR Standard 2-6-4 tank No 80133 at Waterloo, June 1966./*P B Whitehouse*

Below left: Surbiton, 29 May 1951: BR Standard 4-6-2 No 70009 *Alfred the Great* on an up Bournemouth express./*P M Alexander*

Below: The very last express trains to be hauled by steam were the Waterloo to Bournemouth fasts. Here is rebuilt Bulleid Pacific No 34009 *Lyme Regis* at Waterloo on a June morning in 1966./*P B Whitehouse*

Above: Finale: Southern steam in procession in the 150th year celebrations at Shildon in 1975: Bulleid's rebuilt 'Merchant Navy' class 4-6-2 No 35028 *Clan Line.* /Eric Treacy

Below: Bournemouth locomotive shed, June 1967. /P B Whitehouse